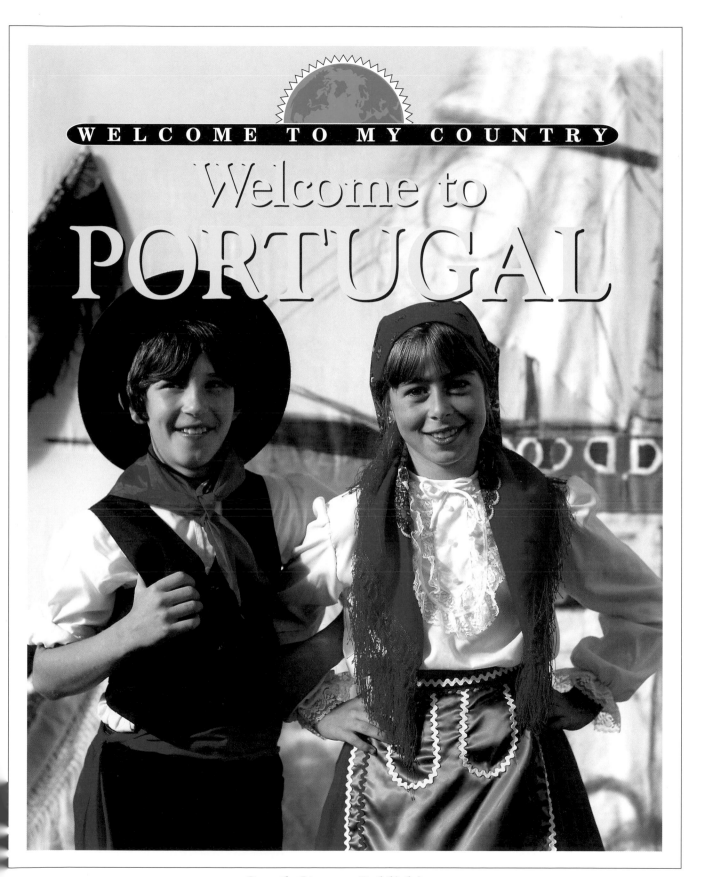

WELCOME TO MY COUNTRY

Welcome to
PORTUGAL

Gareth Stevens Publishing
A WORLD ALMANAC EDUCATION GROUP COMPANY

Written by
ALISON JENSEN/ROSELINE NGCHEONG-LUM

Edited in USA by
DOROTHY L. GIBBS

Designed by
LYNN CHIN

Picture research by
SUSAN JANE MANUEL

First published in North America in 2001 by
Gareth Stevens Publishing
A World Almanac Education Group Company
330 West Olive Street, Suite 100
Milwaukee, Wisconsin 53212 USA

Please visit our web site at
www.garethstevens.com
For a free color catalog describing
Gareth Stevens' list of high-quality books
and multimedia programs, call
1-800-542-2595 (USA) or
1-800-461-9120 (CANADA).
Gareth Stevens Publishing's
Fax: (414) 332-3567.

© **TIMES MEDIA PRIVATE LIMITED 2001**
Originated and designed by
Times Editions
An imprint of Times Media Private Limited
A member of the Times Publishing Group
Times Centre, 1 New Industrial Road
Singapore 536196
http://www.timesone.com.sg/te

Library of Congress Cataloging-in-Publication Data
Jensen, Alison.
Welcome to Portugal / Alison Jensen and Roseline NgCheong-Lum.
p. cm. — (Welcome to my country)
Includes bibliographical references and index.
ISBN 0-8368-2526-8 (lib. bdg.)
1. Portugal—Juvenile literature. [1. Portugal.]
I. NgCheong-Lum, Roseline, 1962– II. Title. III. Series.
DP517.J46   2001
946.9—dc21   2001020230

Printed in Malaysia

1 2 3 4 5 6 7 8 9 05 04 03 02 01

PICTURE CREDITS
A.N.A. Press Agency: 29, 31 (bottom)
Peter Baker/International Photobank: 3 (top),
    9 (bottom), 35, 43, 45
Jan Butchofsky: 4, 6, 11, 30
Focus Team–Italy: 22
Blaine Harrington III: 10, 17
HBL Network Photo Agency: cover, 23, 27
Dave G. Houser: 2, 3 (center), 7, 8, 9 (top),
    19, 25, 26 (bottom), 31 (top), 37
The Hutchison Library: 12
Jason Laure: 1, 5, 14, 18, 20, 21, 32, 38,
    44 (both)
North Wind Picture Archives: 13
Photobank Photolibrary/Singapore: 34
David Simson: 28, 36 (bottom), 41 (top)
Topham Picturepoint: 3 (bottom), 15 (both), 16,
    24, 26 (top), 33, 36 (top), 39, 40, 41 (bottom)

Digital Scanning by Superskill Graphics Pte Ltd

Contents

Words that appear in the glossary are printed in **boldface** type the first time they occur in the text.

Welcome to Portugal!

Portugal is one of the world's oldest independent countries. The nation's long history includes periods of great wealth and power, as well as decades of poverty and political conflicts. Today, Portugal is developing and modernizing. Let's explore Portugal and meet the Portuguese people!

Opposite: The Portuguese often wear traditional costumes to add color to festivals and celebrations.

Below: Since 1999, trains, as well as cars, can cross the Tagus River on Lisbon's April 25th Bridge.

The Flag of Portugal

Portugal's flag has a green and red background with a crest on it. Green stands for hope. Red represents blood shed during the 1910 revolution. The crest symbolizes Portugal's victories over five Moorish kings in the twelfth century.

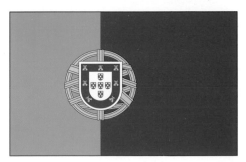

The Land

Portugal is a small country. It has an area of only 35,672 square miles (92,390 square kilometers). The Madeira Islands and the Azores **archipelago** in the Atlantic Ocean are part of Portuguese territory.

Portugal's landscape varies from region to region. Northern Portugal has hills and mountains. The central plains are part of a huge plateau that

Below:
The western part of the Algarve has spectacular rock formations.

covers most of Spain, Portugal's only neighbor. The Algarve, in southern Portugal, has wide, open beaches.

The Tagus River and the Serra de Estrêla mountain range divide northern and southern Portugal. At 6,538 feet (1,993 meters), Torre is the highest mountain on Portugal's mainland. Pico Alto in the Azores, however, is the highest point in all Portuguese territory. It is 7,714 feet (2,351 m) high.

Climate

Northern Portugal has a **temperate** climate, while the southern part of the country is **subtropical**. Sea breezes off the Atlantic Ocean keep summers cool and winters mild in the coastal regions.

Above: Spring brings fields of wildflowers to the Portuguese countryside.

Plants and Animals

More than 2,500 different plant species grow in Portugal. European oak and pine trees are found in the mountainous areas.

Mediterranean trees, such as olive, almond, and cork oak, flourish in the south.

Common animal species include foxes and rabbits. Endangered animals, especially Iberian wolves, lynx, and Mediterranean chameleons, are strictly protected by Portuguese law.

Portugal is on the migration route of many European birds. Spoonbills, avocets, storks, and flamingos are common species all over the country.

Above: In the Alentejo region, storks often build nests on top of chimneys and tall buildings.

Left: Flowering plants thrive in the Algarve. The fertile soil in this region is ideal for almond trees, too.

History

Prehistoric people started to live in Portugal more than 100,000 years ago. The first known group, however, was the Iberians, who settled in Portugal and Spain about 5,000 years ago.

The fiercest Iberians, the Lusitani, tried to fight off the Roman Empire, but they were defeated in 27 B.C. As part of the Roman Empire, Lusitani territory in central Portugal became known as Lusitania.

Left: The ruins of Castelo dos Mouros overlook the town of Sintra in the Lisbon district. This castle was built by the Moors in the eighth or ninth century A.D.

From the Moors to Independence

Roman power declined after 400 A.D. By 711, southern Portugal was controlled by Muslim Moors from North Africa. Northern Portugal held off the Moors and came to be governed by a Spanish kingdom. In 1128, Afonso Henriques declared northern Portugal independent. By 1249, Henriques had freed southern Portugal from Moorish rule. Portugal has been independent ever since.

The Golden Era

In the fifteenth century, Portuguese exploration in Africa, America, and Asia made the country very rich. Vasco da Gama's discovery of a sea route to India in 1498 gave Portugal great maritime power, too. With the gold and other riches from the lands it had conquered, Portugal built some magnificent churches and castles.

The Decline of a World Power

King Philip II of Spain claimed the Portuguese throne in 1580. Under Spanish rule, the country lost much of its power. Even when Spanish rule ended in 1668, Portugal's power continued to decline. In 1826, when Portugal became a **constitutional monarchy**, industry grew, and the country **stabilized**.

Below: When the discovery of gold and diamonds in Brazil boosted Portugal's economy in the seventeenth century, Lisbon harbor became a very busy place.

The Twentieth Century

A revolution in 1910 ended Portugal's constitutional monarchy, and the country became an unstable republic. In 1926, the military took control of the government, and prime minister António Salazar ruled Portugal as a **police state**. The "Carnation Revolution" overthrew the military **regime** in 1974. In the country's first free elections, held in 1976, a **socialist** named Mário Soares was voted Portugal's prime minister.

Below: This **mural** reflects a brief period after the 1974 revolution when **communists** controlled the government in Lisbon.

Henry the Navigator
(1394–1460)

The son of King João I, Prince Henry had a lifelong interest in exploring and colonizing lands across the sea. He also founded a school of navigation in Sagres.

Henry the Navigator

Marquês de Pombal
(1699–1782)

As a minister of King Joseph, Marquês de Pombal governed Portugal from 1750 to 1777. He rebuilt Lisbon after the 1755 earthquake, reorganized the army, and reformed education.

António de Oliveira Salazar
(1889–1970)

As prime minister of Portugal from 1932 to 1968, Salazar ruled Portugal as a **dictator**.

António de Oliveira Salazar

Government and the Economy

Portugal is a republic with an elected parliament and an elected president. The Portuguese parliament, called the Assembly of the Republic, has

254 members. All members of the parliament serve four-year terms. The president, who is the head of state, serves a five-year term. The president chooses a prime minister, as well as a cabinet of ministers.

Above:
Guards on horse-back stand outside the Belem National Palace in Lisbon. The palace is the official residence of Portugal's president.

The Portuguese judicial system has courts ranging from local district and appeals courts to a Supreme Court.

Mainland Portugal is divided into eighteen administrative districts. Each district elects its own governor and has its own legislature.

The European Union

Portugal joined the European Union (EU) in 1986. Although it is the poorest country in the EU, it has gained many important economic benefits with its membership.

Above:
The town hall in Cascais is the summer home of Portugal's president.

Economy

Since Portugal became a member of the EU, manufacturing has been the nation's fastest growing industry. The country manufactures a wide range of products, from textiles and paper to oil and steel.

Portugal's leading **exports** are clothing, footwear, cork, and wine. Its main trading partners are other members of the EU.

Below: The sea is a major source of **revenue** for Portugal. Many Portuguese work in the country's fishing industry.

Natural Resources

Water is one of the most important natural resources in Portugal. The mineral wolframite, which is found in mountainous areas, is another. Uranium is mined in the north, and copper is mined in the south.

Agriculture is also important to the Portuguese economy. The biggest agricultural area is the Alentejo, which is located in central Portugal. Major crops include cork, grapes, and olives.

Above: The post-modern buildings of the Amoreiras business and shopping center in Lisbon were constructed in the 1980s.

People and Lifestyle

Portugal has a population of just over 10 million people. Most Portuguese have dark hair, brown eyes, and olive skin. Their similar appearance is a result of the gradual mixing of the **ethnic** groups that have lived in Portugal over the centuries.

Portugal also has a few minority groups, including Africans, who came from the country's former colonies, and Jews.

Below: People of many different nationalities live and work in big cities such as Lisbon, Oporto, and Coimbra.

Country Life

More than half of the Portuguese population lives in **rural** areas. Since the country **mechanized** in 1986, however, many people have had to move from the fields to the cities to look for work.

Rural lifestyles are determined by seasons and growing cycles. In some parts of northern Portugal, the villagers move to higher pastures with their sheep, cattle, and goats for about five months during the warm season.

City Life

In the **urban** areas of Portugal, most people live in crowded apartment blocks near the center of the city. City dwellers usually take the bus or subway to work because city traffic is so dangerous.

Living Abroad

About four million Portuguese live and work in other countries, especially France, Brazil, and the United States.

They travel to these countries to work because they can earn more money than they would in their homeland. Portuguese **emigrants** usually send some of their earnings back to their families in Portugal.

Families

Family is important to the Portuguese. Most young adults stay in contact with their parents every day, even after they start families of their own.

Education

Compared to other EU countries, the quality of education in Portugal is poor. The number of schools and teachers is not enough for the entire school-age population.

All Portuguese children must complete nine years of elementary education at either a state school, which is free, or a private school, for a fee. Before elementary school,

Left: Founded in 1290, Coimbra University is one of the oldest and most respected universities in the world.

children, ages three to six, may attend preschool. After elementary school, most students go on to a secondary school, but many drop out to go to work.

Students who finish three years of secondary school can continue their education at one of Portugal's eighteen universities, including Coimbra University, or at one of its regional technical colleges.

Above: Students graduating from Coimbra University celebrate with a parade through the city's streets.

Religion

About 95 percent of the Portuguese population is Roman Catholic. About 3 percent belong to other Christian faiths. Christianity was introduced in the first century A.D. Since then, it has been an important part of both Portuguese history and everyday life.

Most Christians go to church every Sunday and celebrate special events, such as baptisms and weddings, in church. Every town and village has

Above: Twice a year, thousands of Roman Catholics travel to Fátima, where, in 1917, three children saw visions of the Virgin Mary.

Left: The Church of Jesus in Setúbal was built in the fifteenth century.

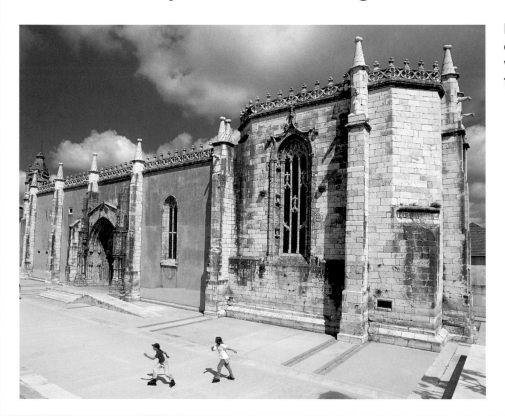

its own patron saint. In some towns, the local church is the center of community life.

Pilgrimages are important to Portuguese Catholics. Popular pilgrimage centers are the shrine at Fátima and the Church of Bom Jesus in Braga.

The number of non-Christians in Portugal is small. Most of them are either Muslim or Jewish.

Language

Like many European languages, Portuguese comes from the Latin spoken by early Roman settlers. Written Portuguese looks like French or Spanish, but spoken Portuguese sounds like Romanian. Pronunciation can be tricky, especially when words contain certain consonant or vowel combinations. Some sounds are slurred, or run together, making them seem "slushy."

Left: The signs at Portugal's popular tourist destinations provide information in both Portuguese and English.

Literature

Portuguese literature dates back to the songs and poems of the twelfth century and includes a lot of writing about the country's history. Portugal's most famous literary work is the epic *The Lusiads*, which was written by Luís Vaz de Camões in 1572. In the twentieth century, Portuguese writers changed the focus of their works to rural life and political themes.

Above: A statue of Portuguese writer Fernando Pessoa stands in front of his favorite café, "A Brasileira," in Lisbon. Pessoa wrote in many styles, and he used a different pen name for each style.

Arts

Painting

Portugal's oldest paintings, the rock art of Foz Côa, date back 25,000 years. As painting developed, Portuguese artists were influenced by French, Flemish, and Spanish styles.

The first widely recognized painter from Portugal was Nuno Gonçalves. Like many Portuguese painters of the

Below:
Special care of sculptures and statues has preserved some of the oldest artwork in Portugal.

fifteenth century, Gonçalves painted only religious subjects, and most of them were portraits. The best-known painter of the twentieth century was Amadeo de Souza Cardoso. His style is called Portuguese Impressionism.

Architecture

Portuguese architecture commonly features low, rectangular designs and elaborately decorated surfaces. In the Portuguese Manueline style, building surfaces are completely covered with wood or stone sculpture.

Music

Bagpipes, harmonicas, flutes, drums, and accordions are instruments that typically accompany traditional Portuguese folk music. Portugal is famous, however, for its stringed instruments, especially the classic twelve-stringed Portuguese guitar. This instrument accompanies a special style of Portuguese music known as *fado* (FAH-doh).

Fado, which started in the 1700s, combines medieval **troubadours'** songs with African slave rhythms.

Left: Fado music is unique to Portugal. This museum in Lisbon is devoted to the history of this musical style.

Although fado songs deal with both joy and sadness, they usually have a sad tone.

Dancing

Portugal has a colorful mix of dance styles that come from the country's different regions and former colonies. Traditional folk dancing is popular throughout Portugal. Each year, the National Folklore Festival in the Algarve attracts music and dance groups from all over the country.

Leisure

The Portuguese like to spend a lot of time with their families. On weekends, they might go to museums or parks, or they might play sports. In towns and villages, men often gather in the evening at local cafés. Women usually meet friends in the afternoon at a tea room or a cake shop.

At home, Portuguese children like to watch television and read. They also like sports. Boys usually play soccer.

Below: In summer, Portugal's beaches are crowded with people enjoying the sand and the sea.

Girls like almost any kind of ball game. Many Portuguese children also belong to groups, such as the Scouts or the Girl Guides.

Bullfighting

Bullfights are popular events in Portugal, but they are not like the bullfights in Spain. A Portuguese bullfighter, or *cavaleiro* (ka-val-EY-roh), performs on horseback and does not kill the bull.

Sports

Soccer is a favorite Portuguese sport, and almost every town and village has its own soccer team. Benfica, FC Porto, and Sporting are the country's most popular teams. The Portuguese national team has competed in many international contests, including the World Cup competition.

Above: Eusebio, Portugal's most famous soccer star, played for the national team at the 1966 World Cup competition.

Portuguese athletes are also strong in track and field events. The country has some of the best marathon runners

in the world. At the 1984, 1988, and 1996 Olympic Games, Portuguese marathon runners won gold medals.

Golf is a popular leisure sport in Portugal. The country has eleven world-class golf courses. Grand Prix car racing is another well-attended sport. Portugal hosts a Formula One Grand Prix every September.

Festivals

Four major festivals in Portugal celebrate historic events. The main holiday, Portugal Day, is held on June 10 in honor of Portuguese poet and **patriot** Luís Vaz de Camões. Republic Day, held on October 5, celebrates the 1910 declaration of the Portuguese republic. Liberty Day on April 25 **commemorates** the "Carnation Revolution." Portugal's Independence Day is December 1.

Below:
On Liberty Day, some Portuguese march through the streets carrying red carnations as reminders of the 1974 revolution that restored **democracy** in Portugal.

Religious Holidays

Holy Week is the most important Christian holiday in Portugal. Grand processions are held throughout the country. Holy Week ends on Easter Sunday. Christmas is an important holiday, too, especially for children. Instead of asking Santa Claus for gifts, however, they ask Baby Jesus. On Christmas eve, almost everyone goes to a midnight church service.

Food

Portuguese **cuisine** is different in each region of the country. Seafood dishes, for example, are common along the coasts. One interesting dish is *cataplana* (ka-ta-PLAN-na), which is a combination of fish and shellfish cooked in a clam-shaped copper pan. People in northern Portugal enjoy pork dishes, including ham and sausages.

Left: Different kinds of shellfish, such as lobsters and crabs, are familiar foods in southern Portugal's Algarve region.

Left: Caldo verde contains smoked sausage, onions, potatoes, and garlic. The soup becomes a green color when shredded cabbage is added in the last stage of cooking.

The most popular food in Portugal is *bacalhau* (bah-kahl-O), which is dried codfish. It can be cooked many ways, including deep-fried, stewed with potatoes, or scrambled with eggs. Another favorite food is *caldo verde* (KAL-do VEHR-duh), which is a green-colored soup.

The Portuguese also love desserts, most of which are made with eggs, almonds, and sugar. Favorite desserts include rice pudding, baked custard, and pastries.

Above: The grapes grown in Portugal are used to make wine. Portugal's three main types of wine are *vinho verde* (VEE-nyo VEHR-duh), port, and Madeira.

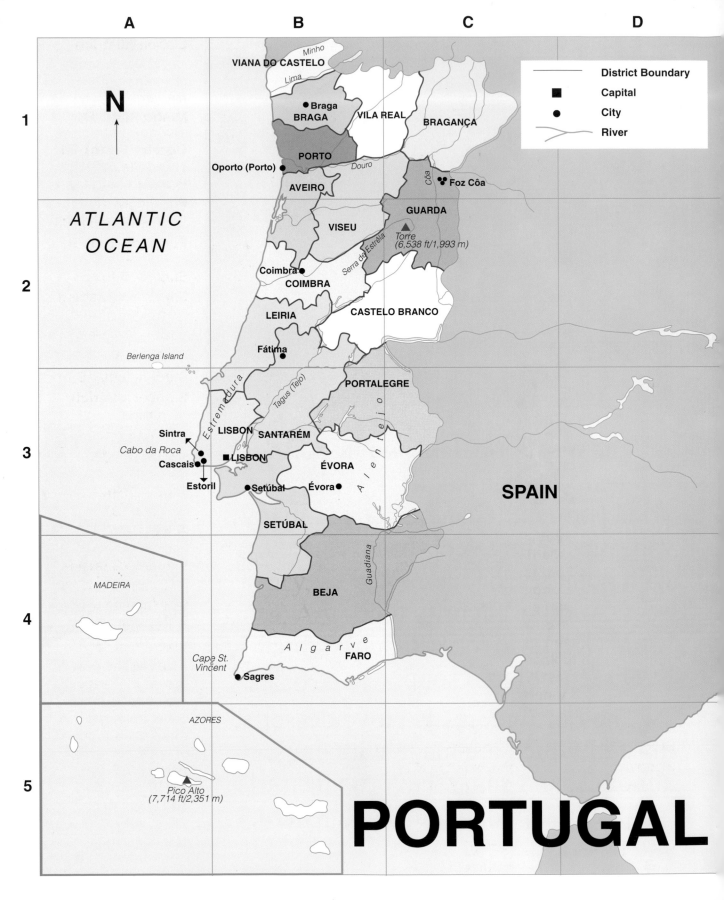

A | B | C | D

N

ATLANTIC
OCEAN

District Boundary
■ Capital
● City
River

Minho
VIANA DO CASTELO
Lima
● Braga
BRAGA
VILA REAL
BRAGANÇA
PORTO
Oporto (Porto) ●
Douro
AVEIRO
Côa
♣♣ Foz Côa
GUARDA
VISEU
▲ *Torre*
(6,538 ft/1,993 m)
Serra da Estrela
Coimbra ●
COIMBRA
LEIRIA
CASTELO BRANCO
Fátima ●
Estremadura
PORTALEGRE
Tagus (Tejo)
Sintra
Cabo da Roca
LISBON
SANTARÉM
Cascais ●
■ **LISBON**
ÉVORA
A l e n t e j o
Estoril
● Setúbal
Évora ●
SPAIN
SETÚBAL
Berlenga Island
Guadiana
MADEIRA
BEJA
A l g a r v e
Cape St. Vincent
FARO
● Sagres
AZORES
▲ *Pico Alto*
(7,714 ft/2,351 m)

PORTUGAL

1

2

3

4

5

Above: The coastal city of Estoril has many beautiful buildings.

Lisbon (district)
A3–B3

Madeira A4
Minho River B1

Oporto (Porto) B1

Pico Alto A5
Portalegre
(district) B2–C3
Porto (district) B1

Sagres B4
Santarém (district)
B2–B3
Serra de Estrêla
B2–C2
Setúbal (city) B3
Setúbal (district)
B3–B4
Sintra A3
Spain C1–D5

Tagus (Tejo)
River B3
Torre C2

Viana do Castelo
(district) B1
Vila Real (district)
B1–C1
Viseu (district)
B1–B2

Alentejo B3
Algarve B4
Atlantic Ocean
A1–C5
Aveiro (district)
B1–B2
Azores A5–B5

Beja (district) B4
Berlenga Island
A2
Braga (city) B1
Braga (district) B1
Bragança
(district) C1

Cabo da Roca A3
Cape St. Vincent
B4

Cascais A3
Castelo Branco
(district) B2–C2
Côa River C1–C2
Coimbra (city) B2
Coimbra
(district) B2

Douro River B1–C1

Estoril A3
Estremadura
A3–B3
Évora (city) B3
Évora (district)
B3–C3

Faro (district) B4
Fátima B2

Foz Côa C1

Guadiana River B4
Guarda (district)
C1–C2

Leiria (district) B2
Lima River B1
Lisbon (city) B3

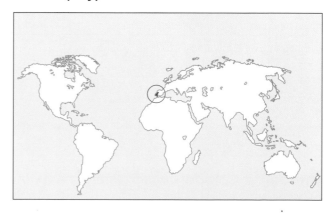

Quick Facts

Official Name	The Republic of Portugal
Capital	Lisbon
Official Language	Portuguese
Population	10,048,232
Land Area	35,672 square miles (92,390 square kilometers)
Districts	Aveiro, Beja, Braga, Bragança, Castelo Branco, Coimbra, Évora, Faro, Guarda, Leiria, Lisbon, Portalegre, Porto, Santarém, Setúbal, Viana do Castelo, Vila Real, Viseu
Highest Point	Pico Alto 7,714 feet (2,351 m) in the Azores archipelago
Longest River	Tagus
Main Religion	Roman Catholicism
Major Festivals	Independence Day (December 1)
	Liberty Day (April 25)
	Portugal Day (June 10)
	Republic Day (October 5)
Currency	Escudos (212.92 escudos = U.S. $1 in 2001)

Opposite: Colorful cockerels are the national emblem of Portugal.

Glossary

archipelago: a chain of islands.

commemorates: remembers or calls to mind.

communists: members of a political system in which the government owns and controls all goods and resources.

constitutional monarchy: a system of government in which a king or sovereign ruler of a nation exercises power according to the laws of an established constitution.

cuisine: a style of preparing and cooking food.

democracy: a system of government by the people in which citizens freely elect their own representatives.

dictator: a ruler who has complete authority over a country.

emigrants: people who leave their home country to live and work in another country.

ethnic: related to a certain race or group of people.

exports: goods sent out of a country to sell in other countries.

mechanized: became equipped with machinery.

mural: a large picture painted directly on a wall or ceiling.

patriot: a person who is loyal to his or her country.

pilgrimages: journeys made to sacred places as an act of religious devotion.

police state: a country in which a national police force, especially secret police, stops any act that goes against government policy.

regime: a system of government; the government currently in power.

revenue: money that comes from sales or taxes and is used to support a government or organization.

rural: related to the countryside.

socialist: related to a political system in which the government owns and controls the country's economy.

stabilized: became firm, steady, or strong.

subtropical: nearby or bordering the hot, damp areas closest to the equator.

temperate: not very hot and not very cold.

troubadours: French court poets.

urban: related to cities or towns.

More Books to Read

Around the World in a Hundred Years: From Henry the Navigator to Magellan. Jean Fritz (Putnam)

The Aztec Empire. Cultures of the Past series. R. Conrad Stein (Benchmark Books)

Portugal. Major World Nations series. Ronald Seth (Chelsea House)

Portugal. Modern Industrial World series. Neil Champion (Thomson Learning)

Portugal in Pictures. Visual Geography series. James Nach (Lerner)

The Travels of Ferdinand Magellan. Explorers and Exploration series. Joanne Mattern (Raintree/Steck Vaughn)

Vasco da Gama and the Portuguese Explorers. Explorers of New Worlds series. Jim Gallagher (Chelsea House)

Videos

Lisbon. Super Cities series. (IVN Entertainment)

Portugal: Southern Coast & Lisbon. Travel the World series. (Questar)

Portuguese Explorers. Explorers of the World series. (Library Video)

Vasco da Gama's Voyage of Discovery. (Kultur Video)

Web Sites

www.algonet.se/~bernadot/christmas/2.html

www.cidadevirtual.pt/mosteiro-jeronimos/vascogamaing.html

www.geocities.com/TheTropics/2140/azores.html

www.newmediarepublic.com/azulejos

Due to the dynamic nature of the Internet, some web sites stay current longer than others. To find additional web sites, use a reliable search engine with one or more of the following keywords to help you locate information about Portugal. Keywords: *fado, Fátima, Gonçalves, Henry the Navigator, Lisbon,* The Lusiads.

Index